X-Ray Tracing

Identifying Latency Bottlenecks

Table of Contents

Chapter 1. Introduction

As our digital world expands and becomes increasingly complex, the propensity for latency bottlenecks in networks becomes a significant concern. This Special Report is dedicated to shedding light on a novel, effective solution, X-Ray Tracing. Despite its highly technical nature, we have made efforts to relay the information in an engaging, accessible manner. Unlocking the mysteries of X-Ray Tracing, this in-depth investigation helps identify latency bottlenecks, focusing on their causes, impacts, and how they can be rectified, all in layman's terms. If your professional life involves battling with pesky network delays or if you're simply intrigued by the dynamics of modern technology, this Special Report promises to enhance your understanding and provide actionable insights. Dive in with us to explore this hidden facet of the digital world.

Chapter 2. Understanding Network Latency: The Bare Basics

In the grand scheme of the digital universe, 'latency' is an often uttered term. However, if you're new to the field, it may seem like a veiled concept. Think of latency as the delay incurred during the transmission of data across a network. This delay typically occurs when information is sent from Point A to Point B and is a crucial determinant of network performance.

2.1. The Genesis of Network Latency

To understand network latency, it is critical to first get a grip on how data transmission works. In the digital world, information doesn't travel in one large bundle but is rather broken down into smaller units, commonly known as 'data packets'. These packets travel through a series of networks or 'nodes' to reach their intended destination.

Here's where latency steps in. It is the time taken by these packets to journey from the source to the destination. It is worth noting that the measure of latency is not only determined by the physical distance that data must traverse but also by how many interim systems or nodes it must pass through.

Imagine a scenario where you're sending a letter from New York to San Francisco via mail. The time it takes for your letter to get there depends not just on the terrestrial distance between the two cities but also on factors like how quickly the postal service processes your letter, how many stops the mail truck makes, and so on. The same concept applies to network latency.

2.2. The Main Culprits Behind Network Latency

There are many factors within a network that can cause latency. The primary three are propagation delay, transmission delay, and processing delay.

1. Propagation Delay: Here, we are dealing with the laws of nature as propagation delay refers to the time it takes for a data packet to travel from one place to another at the speed of light through a physical medium such as fiber optic cable or copper wire. Depending on the medium, propagation speeds can vary. Though not much can be done to alter the speed of light, choosing a medium with faster propagation speeds can reduce this type of delay.

2. Transmission Delay: This involves the delay caused by the time taken to push all the packet's bits onto the network medium. It depends on the packet's size and the data rate of the link. For instance, larger packets and lower data rates increase the transmission delay.

3. Processing Delay: This delay occurs at every node the packet passes through, as the node processes the packet to determine to which link the packet should be sent next. Processing delays can also happen as a node takes time to check for transmission errors, a process that can be exacerbated when the network is congested.

2.3. Corollaries of Network Latency

Latency can impact different applications in different ways. In some cases, high latency could significantly degrade the user experience, while in others, it might not be perceptible.

For real-time communications such as voice and video conferencing, latency plays the villain by causing delay in transmission leading to an echo or unnatural gaps in conversation. In areas such as online gaming, it may cause performance irregularities and lag that could ruin the gaming experience. Similarly, Financial institutions dependent on high-speed trades to make profits would react to increased latency as it equates to lost revenue.

2.4. Mitigating the Latency Menace

Addressing network latency often involves a combination of solutions, both preventive and curative.

Ensuring that your network infrastructure is capable of handling your traffic is critical. Periodic capacity planning, network optimization and modernizing your infrastructure could help in preemptively addressing latency issues. Leveraging modern architectures like Content Delivery Networks (CDNs), which place nodes closer to the user to reduce the distance data needs to travel, could also help in reducing latency.

From a curative standpoint, using network monitoring solutions can help diagnose the point at which latency is introduced into the system. Moreover, these solutions can also help identify patterns, leading to proactive measures to minimize latency.

2.5. X-Ray Tracing: A Beacon of Hope

Amidst this latency riddle, a new technology called X-Ray Tracing promises to unveil the hidden corners of network latency. Instead of focusing solely on delivery, X-Ray Tracing closely dissects network performance to examine packet behavior. The subsequent chapters will delve deeper into the world of X-Ray Tracing, but as an appetizer to that topic, note that it could revolutionize how we comprehend and combat network latency.

Network latency, like many network issues, is a complex beast that requires a strong understand of the underlying mechanics to tame and control. It takes consistent investment of time, resources, and innovative solutions like X-Ray Tracing to overcome. This foray into the bare basics of network latency should provide a concrete foundation as we navigate this intricate and fascinating digital labyrinth.

Chapter 3. Drilling into Latency Bottlenecks: Causes and Effects

Latency, colloquially known as lag, is a prevalent issue in networking. Despite its everyday occurrence, the root causes and effects are often misunderstood by those who are not well versed in networking terminologies and concepts. To make sense of this, we will delve into the depths of latency bottlenecks, inspecting their causes, and exploring their impact on digital systems.

3.1. Understanding the Concept of Latency

Before we delve into the complex world of latency, it is crucial we understand what latency is. In its simplest definition, latency refers to the delay that occurs in a system or network, resulting in the slowdown of data transmission. Latency is measured in milliseconds (ms) and is mostly associated with internet connections but can affect any data transmission system.

When we discuss latency in the context of networks, it is key to understand that data travels in packages across multiple nodes. The time it takes for data to travel from one point to another within a network is known as latency. Any bottleneck that hinders this free movement of data is described as a latency bottleneck.

3.2. Common Causes of Latency Bottlenecks

Latency bottlenecks can occur for a multitude of reasons, and identifying them is the first step towards rectification.

3.3. Impacts of Latency Bottlenecks

Hardware failures: Aging or failing hardware can slow data packet transmission, which can result in increased latency. Regular maintenance and upgrades can help to prevent hardware-induced latency.

The effects of latency bottlenecks can be far-reaching and can impact various components of a digital system.

3.4. Rectifying Latency Bottlenecks

Poor user experience: With digital services, user experience is paramount. High latency can lead to poor user experiences, affecting the reputation of service providers and causing loss of customers.

The first step in rectifying latency bottlenecks is identifying their causes. Once identified, appropriate measures can be adopted to tackle them effectively.

Server-side optimizations: Appropriate server-side optimizations like compression and caching can speed up data processing time, reducing the overall latency experienced by users.

Through understanding and addressing latency bottlenecks, professionals as well as novice users can enhance their network's performance, improving user experience and productivity in the digital world. As we proceed towards an even more interconnected world, being aware of these causes, impacts, and measures to tackle latency bottlenecks becomes not just necessary but imperative. The next chapter will explore the novel solution of X-Ray Tracing in tackling this issue. Stay tuned!

Chapter 4. The Concept of X-Ray Tracing: An Overview

Before diving into the nuances of X-Ray Tracing, it's essential to understand the basic concepts of networking and network latency. Despite being integral to our daily lives, not many appreciate the intricate work of these digital highways. So, what really happens when you press 'Enter' after typing in a URL in your web browser? Your request embarks on a digital journey, at almost the speed of light, through servers, routers, and switches before reaching its destination. Often, this journey is seamless, but occasionally it encounters bottlenecks that delay the response, and that's where the concept of latency steps in.

4.1. Understanding Network Latency

In networking terms, latency refers to the time delay between a request and a response within the network. It's like when you flip a switch and the light takes a moment to turn on. Though the delay is barely noticeable by human standards, in the digital realm, even milliseconds matter. Latency can cost businesses substantial amounts of revenue and customer satisfaction, particularly in sectors where real-time interactions are key, such as gaming, financial trades, and video streaming.

4.2. Enter X-Ray Tracing

In response to the growing threat of network latency, engineers developed the concept of X-Ray Tracing. Much like its namesake in medicine, X-Ray Tracing, in terms of networking, serves to 'visualize' the unseen elements causing delay. It's a diagnostic tool used to identify bottlenecks in the digital pathway of data.

4.3. How X-Ray Tracing Works

Imagine being in an obscure forest; you know your destination, but multiple trails can get you there. Your goal is not just to reach the end but to find the quickest path possible. The conventional way is tedious trial and error, trying every path sequentially.

With X-Ray Tracing, each trail is illuminated all at once, showcasing their lengths metaphorically. Now, picking the shortest becomes easy. Similarly, in the cyber realm, X-Ray Tracing concurrently traces all possible data paths, identifying the shortest and most optimal ones. This allows for quick identification and rectification of latency issues.

Let's break down this process into steps for clarity:

1. Send tracer data packets: The task begins by sending tracer data packets simultaneously down multiple paths within the network. These packets chart and measure the time taken to traverse each route.

2. Collect response data: All tracer packets eventually return to the central probe, or the server where their journey initiated, carrying valuable response time figures.

3. Analytical comparison: The response times are then compared, shedding light on the health of the network. Paths with longer response times indicate potential latency issues.

4. Diagnosis and rectification: Once delay-prone paths are identified, network engineers can diagnose and rectify the issues, optimizing data flow for efficiency.

4.4. Future of X-Ray Tracing

As the digital landscape continues to grow, becoming more complex and interwoven every day, X-Ray Tracing stands on the threshold of becoming an indispensable tool for network management. Its ability to identify and rectify latency issues quickly and accurately makes it a viable solution to ensure that the digital journey of data is as smooth and efficient as possible. X-Ray Tracing is relatively new and promises to evolve in tandem with networking technologies.

Though initially daunting, understanding the concept, its function, and value can empower, benefiting not just those in the tech industry but anyone who engages in the digital world. In the subsequent chapters, we will dig deeper into X-Ray Tracing, exploring its applicability in real-world situations, technical limitations, and its future evolution.

Chapter 5. Working Mechanism of X-Ray Tracing

To understand X-Ray Tracing, it's essential to first get a grasp of the problem it's designed to address.

Computers and networks that work optimally are the backbone of every online operation we today take for granted, whether it's uploading a photo, streaming our favorite Netflix series, or exploring the latest virtual reality gaming experience.

But what happens when that experience is less than smooth? When the photo upload stalls, buffers relentlessly disrupt your cliff-hanger movie, or your vr game lags and crashes, it's the result of what's called latency bottlenecks. Let's delve into the root cause of these nuisance latencies before diving head-on to understand X-Ray Tracing.

5.1. Understanding Latency Bottlenecks

Latency occurs in the network due to unavoidable factors like propagation delays, transmission times, and processing delays. However, these lateness measurements are minimal and typically do not cause substantial slowdowns. The real trouble comes when the Network traffic clogs at certain points, leading to latency bottlenecks, significantly hampering speed and making efficient data transmission impossible.

Latency bottlenecks are congenital to all sorts of networks - local, wide area, or wireless - and are attributable to several technical factors.

1. Network Congestion: Like a busy traffic junction during peak hours, a network can also get congested, causing data packet delays. This congestion typically happens when there are too many data requests compared to the network's bandwidth.

2. Differing Data Pathways: Data packets do not always follow a single pathway. Instead, they travel through different routes, causing disparities in arrival times and leading to buffer bloats.

3. Hardware and Firmware Issues: Sometimes, outdated or substandard hardware and firmware can stall data packets, causing an increase in latency.

To address these latency bottlenecks, technologists have been studying various network tracing tools designed to identify and target latency sources within the network architecture. Among these tools, X-Ray Tracing has emerged as a prominent, effective solution.

5.2. Introduction to X-Ray Tracing

Quite akin to its namesake from the field of healthcare, X-Ray Tracing provides an intricate view into the functioning of network systems, enabling professionals to diagnose where the latency issue lies.

Just as a physician uses an X-ray to view the internal structure of our body and identify any abnormalities, X-Ray Tracing scans through the nooks and crannies of a network set up to identify possible latency bottlenecks.

More precisely, it's a method by which the path taken by a data packet from the source to the destination across the network is traced and documented. It identifies the areas where the data flow is normal and the spots where the slow down (latency) occurs. With the help of such a trace, network administrators can easily identify and rectify bottlenecks.

5.3. How X-Ray Tracing Works

X-Ray Tracing employs a process known as packet tracing. This technique monitors and records the life cycle or route of a data packet through a computer network.

Upon initiation, X-Ray Tracing sends out packets of data, tagged with unique identifying information. This initiator packet then travels through the network, bouncing from server to server as it makes its way to the destination. Every time the packet interacts with a network component (such as a switch or a router), the event gets recorded.

As a result, X-Ray Tracing generates a comprehensive list of actions the packet undergoes in its journey, including:

- The servers, switches, and routers it has interacted with

- The time it has taken at each stop

- Any snares or slowdowns it encountered on its path

This data provides a clear, tangible map of where data transmission might be hanging up from an experience perspective, with the specific components causing the issues and how long these hang-ups last. This concrete and actionable data is what makes X-Ray Tracing a fundamental tool for network management.

5.4. Advantages and Limitations of X-Ray Tracing

Like any technology, X-Ray Tracing has its strengths and weaknesses. Understanding these can help determine when and how to best apply this tool.

The key advantages of X-Ray Tracing are:

1. Detailed View: It offers a detailed window into a network's operations beyond basic connectivity checks. Network administrators can find slow paths, identify high latency devices, and see what network paths are the busiest or least used.

2. Predictive Analysis: By analyzing X-Ray traces over time, it's possible to notice patterns leading to predictable or intermittent latency issues. Thus, future problems can be predicted and avoided.

3. Improved User Experience: By fixing latency bottlenecks and fine-tuning network performance, user experience on any platform, from gaming to streaming to browsing, improves considerably.

Despite its benefits, X-Ray Tracing does entail potential limitations, which include:

1. Resource-Intensive: X-Ray Tracing can be a heavy-duty task, requiring significant system resources to conduct.

2. Overhead: It may add overhead to the network by introducing extra data (packets to be traced).

3. Limited Scope: It might not provide insights into issues occurring outside the traced path, such as firewall configurations or DNS server issues.

Despite these challenges, its ability to provide deep network insights, sturdy diagnostics, and improved network traffic management ensures that X-Ray Tracing maintains an upper hand in our war against latency bottlenecks.

In conclusion, X-Ray Tracing is like peering beneath the surface of the digital world. It charts the flow of data – the life blood of our online existence – through the veins and arteries of network systems, helping us streamline connections, understand discrepancies, remove blockages, and ultimately, have a smoother, faster, and enjoyable digital experience.

Chapter 6. Utilizing X-Ray Tracing: Identifying Latency Bottlenecks

Latency bottlenecks have become an increasing problem in our rapidly digitizing world, resulting in frustrating delays and even leading to significant economic losses. Luckily, a solution is on the horizon: X-Ray Tracing. This breakthrough technique aids in identifying and debugging latency issues, subsequently providing a smoother and more efficient network experience.

6.1. Understanding latency bottlenecks

Before we delve into the workings of X-Ray Tracing, it's vital to clarify what latency bottlenecks are. In layman's terms, latency refers to the delay that occurs in data communication over a network. The longer it takes for a packet of data to travel from one designated point to another, the higher the latency. A bottleneck, in turn, indicates a point of congestion in the data communication pathway leading to a slowdown or halt in the transfer of data. High latency and bottlenecks can seriously impact experiences, particularly as our internet-centric lives demand real-time engagement.

6.2. Bridging the gap with X-Ray Tracing

X-Ray Tracing provides a solution to this contemporary issue. But how exactly? Well, it seamlessly collects and examines data as it moves through a network in real time. It observes how data packets travel from their originating source to their final destination, meticulously recording each tiny delay and hiccup. In doing so, X-Ray Tracing allows us to see the 'inner workings' of our network connections, making the invisible visible.

This ability is incredibly beneficial. For instance, it allows network operators to identify sources of latency, areas of congestion and to rectify these problems proactively. Furthermore, the technique creates an information-rich map of data travel within the network, allowing for analysis and improvement in network performance.

6.3. The science behind X-Ray Tracing

X-Ray Tracing builds on the basic concept of ray tracing, a technique used in physics and other sciences to model the journey of light and other forms of radiation through various mediums. Applying this concept to data, X-Ray Tracing tracks the journey of communication flows throughout the network.

The principle in action here is similar to a doctor using an X-ray to see inside a patient's body without surgery. X-Ray Tracing technology traces each data packet from its source to its final destination across the network, noticing any hang-ups or collisions along the way. In doing so, it's able to pinpoint the locations of latency bottlenecks exactly.

6.4. Implementing X-Ray Tracing: Step-by-step

Begin by priming your network for the X-Ray Tracing operation. This step involves setting up the solution to record data as it passes through the network. Keep in mind that this will require cooperation from all entities involved, as each node needs to be prepared to help 'shine a light' on the data.

Once the data is collected, the 'translating' process begins. This step involves turning raw data into something digestible and interpretable. Note that this step might be the most time-consuming as it involves substantial data processing.

Next, users must 'diagnose' the network. Using the translated data, network operators can identify sources of latency, determine whether an issue is temporary or chronic, and prescribe a course of action.

Lastly, network operators can 'treat' the network. This might be as simple as fine-tuning configurations or as complex as rerouting or dividing traffic flows, but whatever the solution, the data provided by X-Ray Tracing will guide the way.

6.5. Benefits of X-Ray Tracing

It's apparent that X-Ray Tracing is exceptionally beneficial. First and foremost, it provides more visibility into what's happening within the network, which in turn leads to better and more informed decision-making. By highlighting the root causes of latency, it allows for more effective troubleshooting and prevention of repeating issues.

Moreover, X-Ray Tracing has the potential to prevent significant economic losses that can result from lengthy and widespread network downtimes. It can help businesses stay on top of their game in an increasingly digital and interconnected competitive landscape. As more and more businesses migrate to the cloud, the need for such sophisticated network examination tools becomes increasingly crucial.

6.6. In conclusion

As we forge ahead into a progressively digital future, it's becoming critical that we develop sophisticated techniques to manage and maintain our networks. X-Ray Tracing offers a promising solution, enabling us to identify, diagnose and mend latency bottlenecks. By providing a deep, comprehensive view into our networks, it lightens the pathway to a more seamless digital experience. Indeed, X-Ray Tracing may just be the ray of light our digital world needs.

Chapter 7. Case Study: Real-world Application of X-Ray Tracing

In analyzing X-Ray Tracing as a pivotal solution for latency bottlenecks, it's paramount to understand its practical application in real-world scenarios. A comprehensive case study is therefore provided to exhibit the working, advantages and outcomes associated with X-Ray Tracing in an actual network environment.

7.1. The Challenge

Our case revolves around a renowned global company, XYZ Corporation, employing a sprawling network infrastructure. With digital services central to their operations, they house multiple servers worldwide catering to hundreds of thousands of users. However, they grappled with recalcitrant network performance issues - latency bottlenecks being a prime culprit. Complaints of sluggish application responses and interrupted services became a common occurrence.

It became painfully clear that despite the implementation of advanced network monitoring systems, the persistent network latency issues were going unnoticed. These became detrimental to the overall user experience and threatened the corporation's reputation.

7.2. Unmasking the Cause with X-Ray Tracing

Seeking a robust and advanced solution, XYZ Corporation explored the potential of X-Ray Tracing. Armed with the capability to scrutinize their entire network and generate a comprehensive network pathway analysis, the tool seemed promising. It could pinpoint latency issues, regardless of how elusive or intricate.

The team started by deploying the tracer at various points across the global network infrastructure. The tracer, functioning as an inspection tool, traveled along the network pathways, proactively monitoring the traffic flow and interaction between different components.

7.3. The Unforeseen Revelation

As the tracer progressed through the labyrinth of the corporation's network, it revealed bottlenecks unflagged by their current tools. Astonishingly, these were not located where high traffic occurred during peak times as anticipated, instead, they were hidden in corners of the network.

The tracer diligently analyzed each packet's journey, detecting not just the delays but also their causes. There were instances where hardware components weren't optimized for performance and cases of sub-optimal network route configurations contributing to the trouble.

7.4. Implementing Solutions

Armed with detailed insights, the corporation undertook immediate rectification measures. Several hardware components were replaced, network pathways were reconfigured, and priority was given to optimizing servers handling extensive data.

After several rounds of optimizations, they once again set the X-Ray Tracing tool to work, double-checking the effectiveness of the implementation. This time, the tracer coursed through the network, reporting significantly reduced latency times and almost no bottlenecks.

7.5. Seeing the Results

Post-optimization, the user complaints regarding slow applications and service interruptions dropped considerably. This was soon reflected in their customer satisfaction surveys, showing a palpable boost in ratings. The company also noted a rise in productivity, with employees able to complete tasks without battling network delays.

7.6. The Takeaway

This case study testifies to the high potential of X-Ray Tracing. The tool proved instrumental in detecting otherwise elusive latency bottlenecks in an intricate network, thereby driving swift rectification and leading to enhanced network performance and satisfaction across the board.

X-Ray Tracing may seem daunting or excessive initially, but deploying this technology can profoundly enhance the overall network experience. It promotes better understanding and control of one's network, helping identify bottlenecks, and provides meaningful, actionable insights into addressing latency problems, thereby ensuring a high-quality digital experience.

Whether you're a business grappling with network delays or an individual curious about this transformative technology, X-Ray Tracing provides an effective, valuable solution. As our case study of XYZ Corporation reveals, this tool doesn't just detect bottlenecks, it shines a light on the entire journey of the network data - a step that's integral to optimizing our digital world.

Chapter 8. Interpreting the Results: Decoding X-Ray Tracing Reports

X-Ray Tracing is a powerful tool designed to help alleviate latency issues within a network. Much like a doctor uses an X-ray machine to look into the body, X-Ray Tracing provides a way to probe into a network and identify issues causing latency. But to truly utilize this tool, one needs to know how to interpret the results it provides. This isn't as formidable a task as it may appear. In fact, with the right understanding, decoding X-Ray Tracing reports can actually become a straightforward process.

8.1. Understanding the X-Ray Tracing Terminology

Before we venture into understanding detailed reports, it's worth familiarizing ourselves with some basic terminology. X-Ray Tracing utilizes four major types of data packets to facilitate its operation:

1. Inject: Initiate the testing process.

2. Acknowledge: Confirm receipt of data.

3. Trace: Contain the trace data being analyzed.

4. Goodbye: Terminate the testing process.

These communications are reflected in the reports you'll be reading once the trace is completed.

8.2. The Breakdown of an X-Ray Tracing Report

After running a tracing operation, you will be provided with a comprehensive report. Here's what a typical section might look like, explained in plain English:

- Host: This is the server or the device on which the trace was run.

- Trace Time: The duration in which the X-Ray Tracing was performed.

- Packets Sent: Total data packets that were sent.

- Packets Received: The packets that made it back.

- Lost Packets: The packets that never returned.

Each packet's journey is recorded, along with latency, denoting how long it took for each packet to get from its sending point to its destination and back. High latencies are usually bad news. It means data is taking a long time to travel, indicating possible bottlenecks or other complications.

8.3. Isolating Problematic Areas

Now that you have a basic understanding of the report elements, it is time to learn how to identify potential issues within your network infrastructure.

The first data to consider is the lost packets. A large number of lost packets is usually indicative of a problem. Ideally, this number should be as close to zero as possible.

High latencies should also raise a red flag. You want to see a low average for the round trip times. Latency distribution can give key insights. If the round trip times for a large percentage of packets exceed the average, then you might have a congested network or some physical limitations causing delays.

8.4. Understanding Trace Paths

Trace Paths are also recorded in the X-Ray Tracing report and could be a goldmine of information. Tracing the path of the packets from the source to the destination can help identify specific nodes or links within the network where issues might occur.

The Trace Path section may also include the following:

- Hop: Refers to a router or a gateway in the journey of the packet.

- Round Trip Time: The time taken for the packet to travel from the source to the destination and back.

- Address: The IP address of the particular hop.

- Packet Loss: The percentage of packets that were lost during the trip to this hop and back.

8.5. Taking Action

Once you've identified the presence of latency issues, it's crucial to address them. This might require further investigation, potentially bringing in a networking professional for more complex issues. It might also mean reaching out to your internet service provider if you suspect the issue lies outside your internal network.

Remember, X-Ray Tracing is an incredibly powerful tool, and the report is an invaluable resource in the quest to minimize or eradicate latency. By understanding how to read these comprehensive reports, you arm yourself with invaluable knowledge. Not only can you find out where the problems lie, but you can also observe whether changes you're making are having the desired effects.

In conclusion, the utility of X-Ray Tracing becomes clear only when its results can be efficiently decoded and interpreted. Remember to regularly consult your reports in order to keep your network healthy and latency-free. Happy tracing!

Chapter 9. The Role of X-Ray Tracing in Network Optimization

In an age of hyper-connectivity, smooth and uninterrupted network performance is not just a nicety—it's a necessity. Understanding every bit and byte, every nanosecond that could make a difference, comes into play. This is where X-Ray Tracing, a revolutionary approach, comes into the picture.

9.1. Understanding X-Ray Tracing

Drawing an analogy from its medical namesake, X-Ray Tracing is about looking beneath the surface. However, instead of evaluating bone structures and body tissues, this technique focuses on investigating the health of network pathways. By monitoring and measuring the minuscule data-led conversations that happen over the network, X-Ray tracing aids in gaining a comprehensive understanding of its dynamics.

A novelty in the network optimization realm, X-Ray Tracing can 'see' and 'record' interactions between different network components. It operates by sending out packets of information from one end of the infrastructure to another, tracking their journey, and visually plotting their path. This provides a full, unobstructed view of how information flows through a system and highlights any points of congestion or latency.

9.2. X-Ray Tracing Versus Traditional Approaches

Traditional network performance monitoring tools provide an outside-looking-in perspective. These tools monitor servers, interfaces, routers, and other network devices for performance counters or SNMP (Simple Network Management Protocol) metrics to determine their health and status.

However, while traditional tools can identify that there's an issue with latency or network speed, they fall short in precisely identifying where the problem lies.

That's where X-Ray Tracing proves to be a game-changer, taking an inside-out view, tracing packets of data as they transit the network, logging every stop, pause, redirection, or detour. This way, it accurately pinpoints where delays and bottlenecks occur, thus making way for operations teams to intervene and take corrective measures.

9.3. How X-Ray Tracing Works

In essence, X-Ray Tracing functions by sending tracer packets across the network, tracking their journey, and providing detailed visibility into their path. The steps involved are:

1. Emission: The tracing procedure begins with a 'tracer packet' created and sent on its way through the network. This packet serves as our 'X-Ray', lighting up the infrastructure's dark corners.

2. Tracing: As the tracer packet traverses the network, it logs every interaction—every router it passes through, every switch it encounters. Each stop or redirect, delay or reroute, is meticulously logged and time-stamped.

3. Visual Map: Once the tracer packet completes its journey, the resulting logs are used to create a detailed and visual map of the packet's path, highlighting any points of latency or delay.

Thereafter, real user monitoring data is analyzed alongside these tracing reports to identify common patterns of delay or under-performance. This helps to create a holistic overview of network performance and provides clear, actionable insights.

9.4. Barriers to the Adoption of X-Ray Tracing

Despite the clear benefits of X-Ray Tracing, adoption has its challenges. High resource consumption is one of the foremost concerns, as the process of tracing every packet of data and logging their journey can strain server resources. This is where effective workload balancing and cloud-based solutions come into play, offsetting the strain on servers.

Another barrier is education and understanding. Given the novelty of the technology, there may be resistance in its adoption, particularly among conventional organizations. One way to overcome this is to intensify educational and outreach initiatives, as well as providing businesses with easy-to-digest, visual representations of how X-Ray Tracing can enhance their network performance.

9.5. The Future of Network Optimization: X-Ray Tracing

In closing, as our reliance on robust and 'always-on' networks grows, network optimization techniques, like X-Ray Tracing, are set to take center stage. By precisely pinpointing the sources of latency and bottlenecks, X-Ray Tracing enables an unprecedented level of clarity and control over network infrastructure.

With artificial intelligence (AI) and machine learning (ML) advancements, we anticipate that X-Ray Tracing will become smarter, learning from past tracer patterns to predict and pre-empt future issues.

Regardless of some challenges in adoption, X-Ray Tracing has the potential to significantly change the landscape of network optimization, providing an exciting frontier to explore. In this rapidly digitalizing world, not only does X-Ray Tracing stand as an effective solution for latency bottlenecks, but it also foreshadows a future where networks can be fully transparent, truly optimized, and perpetually ready to support our ever-growing digital aspirations.

Chapter 10. Advanced X-Ray Tracing Techniques: Going Beyond the Basics

While the fundamental principles of X-Ray Tracing simplifies the identification and mitigation of network latency, embracing advanced techniques empower network professionals to circumnavigate persistent and complex bottlenecks. This chapter sheds light on these flourishing techniques, and how they interconnect to showcase their potential to realize proactive latency management.

10.1. The Role of Heatmaps in X-Ray Tracing

An accessible visualization tool for X-Ray Tracing is the heatmap. Heatmaps help locate and quantify latency bottlenecks by illustrating the geographical distribution of network traffic and latency delays. Each pixel on the heatmap corresponds to a network node and is colored to represent the latency time: high latency nodes are colored red, while green nodes have low latency.

Heatmaps not only offer a perceptual view of latency across the network but could also showcase patterns of latency occurrence. This understanding could subsequently aid in scheduling necessary infrastructure improvements or rerouting network traffic during peak usage times to more efficient routes.

Clock resolution plays a critical role here – the lower the resolution, the more detailed your heatmap. Understanding how to scale resolution to your specific network needs is vital to maximizing the utility of heatmaps in your network analysis.

10.2. Progressive Photon Mapping in X-Ray Tracing

Following the heatmap visualization, the notion of Progressive Photon Mapping (PPM) comes into play. PPM is a global illumination algorithm used in X-Ray Tracing to improve the precision of network analysis by progressively enhancing the resolution as photons, representing data packets, are traced across the network.

To make this more understandable: A larger concentration of photons at a certain node signifies higher usage or traffic, which might result in greater latency. Thereby, applying PPM to X-Ray Tracing allows for a more nuanced understanding of the nodes contributing most to network latency.

Advanced X-Ray Tracing implements PPM in phases; the first phase gathers network traffic information, and the subsequent phases gradually refine this information. This technique is beneficial in driving more precise detection and mitigation of latency bottlenecks, especially in larger networks where data packets follow complex routes.

10.3. Temporal Coherence Utilization

Once an understanding of the critical latency-contributing nodes is established, the next step could be examining the 'temporal coherence' of these nodes. Temporal Coherence is the concept that consequently captured frames (or network states) are likely to be similar.

The assumption is adjoining network states share similar latency characteristics. As a consequence, X-Ray Tracing can utilize information provided by previous network states to predict future states, with an aim to identify and manage potential latency bottlenecks proactively.

Leveraging Temporal Coherence can optimize X-Ray Tracing processes by reducing the computational load. If latency characteristics do not alter significantly from one state to another, pulling data from prior states mitigates the need for expansive network analysis for each individual state. This practice saves computational resources and enhances overall network efficiency.

10.4. Advanced Monte Carlo Techniques

The convergence of advanced X-Ray Tracing with sophisticated Monte Carlo techniques has taken network latency analysis a notch higher. Leveraging probabilistic models, Monte Carlo methods provide a deeper, more accurate depiction of how data packets journey throughout your network.

These methods simulate the movement of packets across the network, facilitating the detection of potential latency bottlenecks by predicting how packets might interact with individual network nodes. Besides, Monte Carlo techniques afford the ability to foresee potential latency concerns under different network conditions by altering input parameters in the simulation model.

They are crucial tools when dealing with larger networks where traditional methods become excessively time-consuming or technically impractical. Though they demand more computational resources, their usage leads to sharper, more actionable insights that help in effectively managing and mitigating latency concerns.

Each of these advanced techniques plays an indispensable role in enhancing the effectiveness of X-Ray Tracing in network latency analysis, bringing it closer to the ideal of real-time, predictive, and proactive network management. Balancing these methods according to the particular requirements of the network could deliver better latency mitigation, lead to improved network functionality, and reduce latency-induced frustrations down the lane.

Chapter 11. The Future of X-Ray Tracing: Predictions and Possibilities

The future of X-Ray Tracing hinges on its ability to evolve dynamically within the rapidly shifting technological landscape. In order to predict the trajectory of X-Ray Tracing and its potential, we need to first understand the associated challenges, the innovative developments, and the wide range of applications to which it can be applied.

11.1. The Current Challenges

While advancements in X-Ray Tracing have enabled us to peek into the intricate behind-the-scenes of network operations, several challenges abound.

The sheer complexity of networks, for one, continues to be a high wall to scale. As networks expand alongside digital progress, their complexity inevitably increases. Larger networks imply more elements to consider, making the task increasingly demanding for X-Ray Tracing tools.

Another obstacle relates to real-time network monitoring. Current network infrastructure might not always support the monitoring granularity required by X-Ray Tracing tools. This poses a challenge in achieving seamless, real-time latency detection and rectification.

Feature development poses one more hurdle. The ideal X-Ray Tracing tool should be capable of autonomous learning and adjustment, potentially through Machine Learning or AI. However, implementing such capabilities while ensuring data privacy and security concerns can be daunting.

11.2. The Advancing Innovations

Despite these challenges, the technology and innovation space doesn't cease to evolve and adapt. New advancements in X-Ray Tracing show a promising trajectory for overcoming these difficulties.

First and foremost, an increasing focus on hybrid network environments promises a significant upgrade to traditional network setups. With a hybrid network, combining wired and wireless networks, the broadened range and reachability allow for a more comprehensive application of X-Ray Tracing.

Cloud computing is another avenue where X-Ray Tracing could shine brighter. The current trend toward virtualization, specifically Network Function Virtualization (NFV), provides an almost sandbox-like environment, permitting X-Ray Tracing tools to investigate latency issues in a controlled manner.

Additionally, the rise of Machine Learning and AI advents provides apt solutions regarding feature development. Machine Learning algorithms can train X-Ray Tracing tools to become more sophisticated, learning from past data to predict and address future network latency issues.

11.3. Predicted Applications

The potential applications of X-Ray Tracing are expansive and span various sectors. These include but are not limited to e-commerce, the Finance Sector, Telecommunication, Online Gaming, Autonomous Vehicles, and 5G Networks.

E-commerce platforms could leverage X-Ray Tracing to uncover latency issues, thus boosting customer service and enhancing the overall user experience. The Finance sector could similarly benefit, using X-Ray Tracing to ensure swift and smooth financial transactions, a critical aspect of their service.

Telecommunications could boost their Quality of Service (QoS), offering consumers faster, more reliable network services. Online Gaming platforms could improve the player experience, reducing in-game lags, a common source of frustration among gamers.

A field that could potentially see a leap in progress through X-Ray Tracing is Autonomous Vehicles. By ensuring seamless communication between vehicles, and between vehicles and external servers, X-Ray Tracing could significantly enhance vehicle response times, thus contributing to safer and more efficient road networks.

Anticipating the dawn of 5G technology, X-Ray Tracing could play a substantial role in optimizing this advanced form of telecommunications. By identifying and rectifying network latency bottlenecks, it could ensure the true, promised potential of 5G is realized, delivering extremely fast, reliable, and high-capacity networks.

11.4. Future Possibilities

The possibilities for X-Ray Tracing's evolution are practically limitless. At the junction of our current reality and science fiction, we see horizon technologies such as Quantum Computing. How X-Ray Tracing adapts within quantum networks is an exciting frontier, one promising mind-bending speed and efficiency.

We also see a future toward multi-mode network latency detection and rectification. As X-Ray Tracing tools become more refined, they could simultaneously process multiple latency types across various network infrastructures. This would result in an advanced, integrated tool that could effectively combat a wide spectrum of network latency bottlenecks.

In conclusion, the future of X-Ray Tracing appears dynamic, challenging and exciting. Admittedly, obstacles exist. However, as the technology landscape evolves, X-Ray Tracing will likely adapt and overcome these challenges, carving a niche in the increasingly interconnected realm of tomorrow. An end to annoying network latencies seems not just possible but probable, with X-Ray Tracing pioneers leading the charge.

9 798856 421391